KANJI
de MANGA
Vol. 2

MANGA UNIVERSITY presents...

The Comic Book That Teaches You How To Read And Write Japanese!

volume 2

 Created by Glenn Kardy  Art by Chihiro Hattori

Japanime

TOKYO   SAN FRANCISCO

Manga University Presents ... Kanji de Manga
The Comic Book That Teaches You
How To Read And Write Japanese
Volume Two

Published by Manga University under the auspices of Japanime Co. Ltd.,
3-31-18 Nishi-Kawaguchi, Kawaguchi-shi, Saitama-ken 332–0021, Japan.

www.mangauniversity.com

ISBN-13: 978-4-921205-03-4
ISBN-10: 4-921205-03-5

07 08 09 10   10 9 8 7 6 5 4

Printed in Canada

CONTENTS

Introduction 7

Study Section 11

Practice Section 93

Kanji Index 138

 **INTRODUCTION**

Welcome to the second volume of *Kanji de Manga*, your guide to the exciting world of Japanese writing.

If you're reading this book, you probably already know the first 80 basic Japanese kanji characters. Maybe you learned them by studying the first book in our *Kanji de Manga* series. Perhaps you picked them up on a trip to Japan. Or maybe you studied some Japanese in school.

No matter how you learned them, give yourself a pat on the back—you're well on your way to learning the most difficult part of the Japanese language. And now you're ready for a new and stimulating challenge as you continue your journey.

By now, you've probably figured out a few things. First, that all those warnings were true: learning kanji is truly challenging. But at the same time, we hope you've found that it's not as difficult as you feared it might be—and that it really can be fun to learn Japanese through manga.

Secondly, you've probably already seen how far those 80 basic kanji can take you. Maybe for the first time you saw a sign in Japanese and instantly knew what it meant. Or perhaps you were able to read parts of a Japanese comic book.

And finally, you're probably starting to see how some of the basic strokes reappear in many different characters, and learning these strokes already has taken some of the mystery out of Japanese writing.

Now you're ready for the next step. And while it's still going to be challenging, it's going to be even more rewarding because in the end, you'll know twice as many characters!

In this book, we'll teach you 80 of the kanji that are needed to pass the third level of the Japanese Language Proficiency Test. (For more information about the test, please see page 92.) In Japan, these characters are taught between the first and fourth grades of grammar school.

Combined with the 80 characters you've already learned from the first volume (you *have* learned them by now, right?), the 160 kanji that will be part of your life when you reach the end of this book will take you deep into the world of Japanese writing.

And when you're ready for the next step, the next edition of *Kanji de Manga* will be there to help you through it.

So get those pens ready... *Gambatte!*

PAGE GUIDE

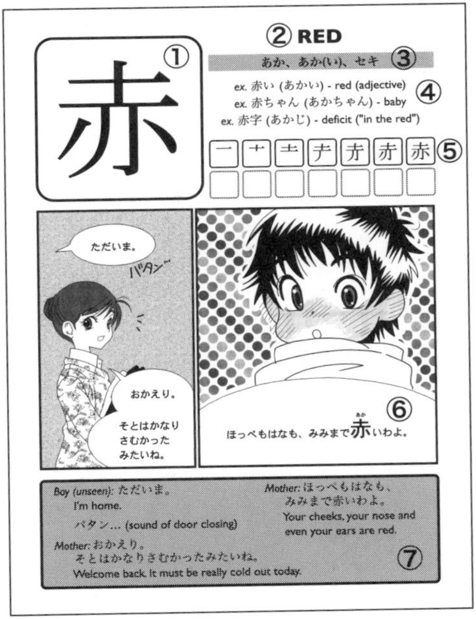

赤 ①
② RED
あか、あか(い)、セキ ③
ex. 赤い (あかい) - red (adjective)
ex. 赤ちゃん (あかちゃん) - baby
ex. 赤字 (あかじ) - deficit ("in the red") ④
⑤
ただいま。
バタン
おかえり。
そとはかなりさむかったみたいね。
⑥
ほっぺもはなも、みみまで赤いわよ。
Boy (unseen): ただいま。
I'm home.
バタン… (sound of door closing)
Mother: おかえり。
そとはかなりさむかったみたいね。
Welcome back. It must be really cold out today.
Mother: ほっぺもはなも、みみまで赤いわよ。
Your cheeks, your nose and even your ears are red.
⑦

① The featured kanji

② Common definition

③ Readings: kun-yomi (Japanese readings) are written in hiragana, while on-yomi (Chinese readings) are in katakana.

④ Examples of compounds containing the featured kanji, their pronunciations (written in hiragana) and English definitions. (An asterisk next to a compound indicates that one or more of its kanji are not featured in this or the first volume of the "Kanji de Manga" series.)

⑤ Stroke order: In general, the strokes are written from top to bottom and left to right. For a list of additional stroke-order rules, please refer to the chart at the back of this book.

⑥ The manga. All dialogue is written in hiragana and katakana except for the single featured kanji. The proper pronunciation of the kanji is indicated in furigana (tiny hiragana) written above the character.

⑦ Translation of the dialogue and selected onomatopoeia.

Kanji de Manga

けんじくんて勉きょう
ねっしんね。

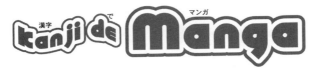

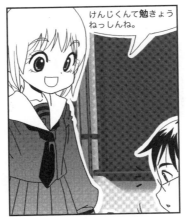

STUDY SECTION

MEET / SOCIETY

あ(う)、カイ

ex. 会社 (かいしゃ) - company
ex. 社会 (しゃかい) - society
ex. 会話 (かいわ) - conversation

あれ？

うわー！
ひさしぶり。
げんきだった？

こんなところで
会うなんておどろいたわ！

Girls (together): あれ？
Huh?

Girl on left: うわー！ひさしぶり。げんきだった？
Wow! Long time, no see. How have you been?

Girl on right: こんなところで会うなんておどろいたわ！
I'm so surprised to meet you here!

BLUE

青

あお、あお(い)、セイ

ex. 青空 (あおぞら) - blue sky
ex. 青天 (せいてん) - fine weather
ex. 青い鳥 (あおいとり) - bluebird

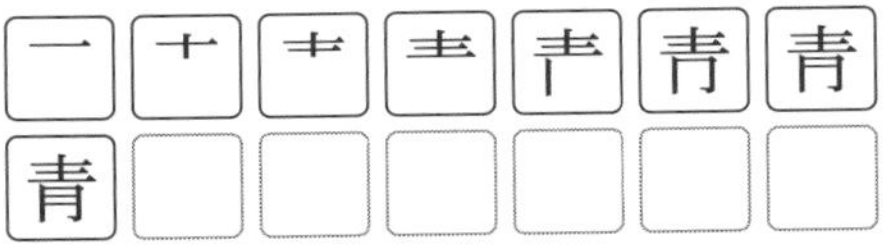

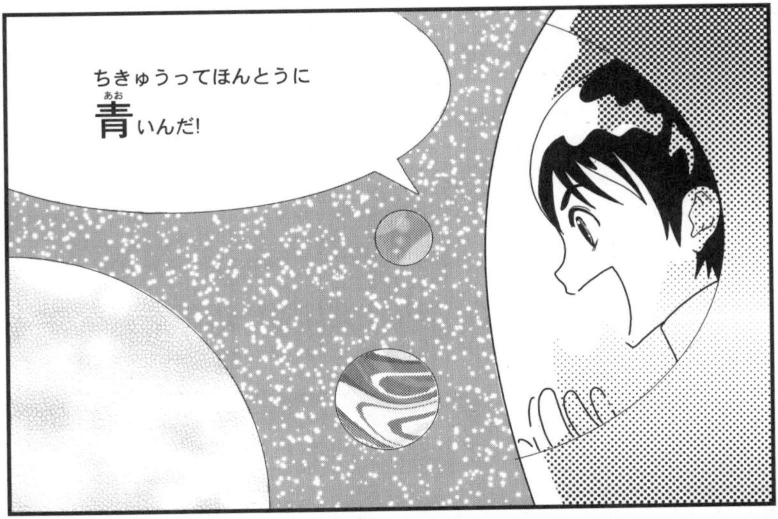
ちきゅうってほんとうに
青(あお)いんだ!

Astronaut: ちきゅうってほんとうに青いんだ！
The earth really is blue!

赤

RED

あか、あか(い)、セキ

ex. 赤十字 (せきじゅうじ) - The Red Cross
ex. 赤ちゃん (あかちゃん) - baby
ex. 赤字 (あかじ) - deficit ("in the red")

ただいま。
バタン
おかえり。
そとはかなり
さむかった
みたいね。

ほっぺもはなも、みみまで赤いわよ。

Boy (unseen): ただいま。
I'm home.

バタン… (sound of door closing)

Mother: おかえり。
そとはかなりさむかったみたいね。
Welcome back. It must be really cold out today.

Mother: ほっぺもはなも、
みみまで赤いわよ。
Your cheeks, your nose and even your ears are red.

BRIGHT / CLEAR

明

あか(るい)、あき(らか)、メイ、ミョウ

ex. 明日 (あした) - tomorrow
ex. 明月 (めいげつ) - full (bright) moon
ex. 文明 (ぶんめい) - civilization

どうか、明すの ぶんかさいは、 はれますように!
ぜったい、明すの ぶんかさいは、 はれてほしい!
てるてるぼうずおねがい。 どうか はれますように。

Girl: どうか、明すのぶんかさいは、はれますように！
Please let it be sunny for tomorrow's Culture Festival!

ぜったい、明すのぶんかさいは、はれてほしい！
Pleeeaaassseee let it be sunny for tomorrow's Culture Festival!

てるてるぼうずおねがい。どうかはれますように。
Teruterubozu,* please let it be sunny.

*A teruterubozu is a paper doll to which Japanese children pray for good weather.

秋

AUTUMN

あき、シュウ

ex. 秋口 (あきぐち) - beginning of autumn
ex. 秋分 (しゅうぶん) - autumn equinox
ex. 秋風 (あきかぜ) - autumn wind

どうしたんだろう…ためいきなんかついて…
秋はやっぱりものがなしくなるのかなぁ…
うんうん
ロマンチックだもんな。
おなかすいた…
はぁぁ…
かんどう!

Girl: ふう… (sigh)

Boy: どうしたんだろう…ためいきなんかついて…
What's up... Why the long face...

Boy: 秋はやっぱりものがなしくなるのかなぁ…
Autumn does make one feel melancholy...

うんうん Yes, yes...

ロマンチックだもんな。
It's a romantic time.

Girl: おなかすいた…
I'm hungry...

はぁぁ (sigh)

Boy: かんどう！
I'm impressed!

MORNING

あさ、チョウ

ex. 今朝 (けさ) - this morning
ex. 明朝 (みょうちょう) - tomorrow morning
ex. 朝食 (ちょうしょく) - breakfast

一	十	广	古	古	直	直
卓	卓	朝	朝	朝		

どうしたの？
朝からちょうし
わるそうよ。

ふあ～…

まあね…

じつは朝までずっと
ほんをよんでいてあまり
ねていないんだ。

……

ガ
ク…

すいりものでさ。
とまらないんだ、
これが…

Schoolgirl: どうしたの？
朝からちょうしわるそうよ。
What's wrong? You've seemed
sick since the morning.

Schoolboy: まあね… Yeah...

ふあ～… (yawn)

Schoolboy: じつは朝までずっとほんを
よんでいてあまりねていないんだ。
Actually, I was reading a book till morning
and didn't sleep.

Schoolgirl: (speechless) がく (sound of shock)

Schoolboy: すいりものでさ。とまらないんだ、
これが… It was a mystery. I couldn't put it down...

FOOT / LEG

あし、たり(る)、たる、ソク

ex. 足早 (あしばや) - quick-footed
ex. 足跡* (あしあと) - footprint
ex. 足袋* (たび) - Japanese-style socks

むむっ!

ゆかにどろの
足あと?!

だぁれ? 足のうらがよごれているのは?!

足を
あらいなさい!

Mother: むむっ!
Hey!

ゆかにどろの
足あと?!
Muddy footprints all
over the floor?!

Mother: だぁれ? 足のうらがよごれているのは!
足をあらいなさい!
Who? Who is the one with the dirty feet?!
Go wash your feet now!

ELDER BROTHER

あに、キョウ、ケイ

ex. 兄嫁* (あによめ) - elder brother's wife
ex. 兄弟 (きょうだい) - siblings
ex. 父兄 (ふけい) - parents; guardians

丨 丨 冂 口 尸 兄

また
にんじんのこして!

だって、
きらいなんだもん。

お兄ちゃんの
ようにつよく
なれないわよっ。

ムキ
ムキ

お兄ちゃん
みたいになんか
なりたくないよ!

Mother: また
にんじんのこして！
You haven't eaten your
carrots again!

Girl: だって、
きらいなんだもん。
Because I hate them.

Mother: お兄ちゃんのように
つよくなれないわよっ。
They'll make you strong like your big brother.

ムキムキ (sound of flexing muscles)

Girl: お兄ちゃんみたいになんかなりたくないよ！
But I don't want to be like him!

姉

ELDER SISTER

あね、シ

ex. 姉妹 (しまい) - sisters
ex. お姉さん (おねえさん) - young lady
ex. 姉妹都市* (しまいとし) - sister cities

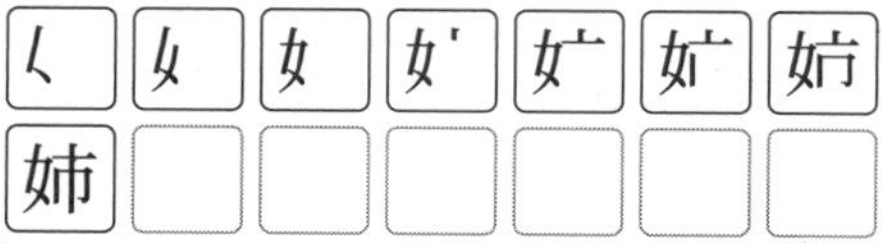

おぎゃーっ
おぎゃーっ
ぼしともにけんこうなおとこのこですよ。
ほっ
おとうとだぞ。
きょうからお姉(ねえ)ちゃんだね。
うん!

おぎゃーっ
おぎゃーっ (baby crying)

Nurse: ぼしともにけんこうな
おとこのこですよ。
Mother and baby are doing fine.

Father: ほっ Whew...

Nurse: おとうとだぞ。
きょうからお姉ちゃんだね。
It's a boy. Now you're a big sister.

Little girl: うん！
Yup!

WALK

ある(く)、あゆ(む)、ホ、ポ、ブ

ex. 歩道 (ほどう) - sidewalk; footpath
ex. 一歩一歩 (いっぽいっぽ) - step by step
ex. 歩兵* (ほへい) - foot soldier; infantryman

歩

ね、このあと こうえんで さん歩(ぽ)でも しない?
いいわね。

みどりのなかを 歩(ある)くのって きもちいいよね。
さん歩(ぽ)って いいわね。

College student: ね、このあと こうえんでさん歩でもしない?
Hey, you wanna go for a stroll in the park?

Roommate: いいわね。
Good idea.

College student: みどりのなかを 歩くのってきもちいいよね。
It feels wonderful to walk outdoors.

Roommate: さん歩っていいわね。
Yeah, walks are great.

SAY / SPEECH

い(う)、こと、ゲン、ゴン

ex. 言語 (げんご) - language
ex. 言い合い* (いいあい) - quarrel; dispute
ex. 言葉* (ことば) - word(s); speech

おとこらしく
はっきりと
言ったら?

...す
すっ
......

Schoolgirl: おとこらしくはっきりと言ったら？
Why don't you be a man and tell me what
you want to say?

Schoolboy: ...す
すっ......
(stuttering)

Schoolboy: すきだ
I like you!

ポッ (sound of surprise)

HOUSE / FAMILY

いえ、や、カ、ケ

ex. 家族* (かぞく) - family
ex. 家内* (かない) - household; wife
ex. 家計* (かけい) - housekeeping

え?!じぶんで
家をたてたの?!

家っていっても、

ポチの
家だけど...

すごい
すごい!

わん

わん

Sister: え？！じぶんで
家をたてたの？！
Huh?! You built a house
all by yourself?!

Brother: 家っていっても、ポチの家だけど...
Well, yeah, a house, but just Pochi's doghouse...

Sister: すごいすごい！
Wow! Wonderful!

Dog: わんわんわん
Woof, woof

犬

DOG

いぬ、ケン

ex. 犬小屋* (いぬごや) - doghouse; kennel
ex. 猟犬* (りょうけん) - hunting dog
ex. 犬かき (いぬかき) - dog paddle (swim)

一	ナ	大	犬			

いぬ
犬って
かわいいわね!
いぬ
犬って
かわいいと
おもわない?
そ…
そうだね…

Girl: 犬ってかわいいわね！
Dogs are so cute!

Girl: 犬ってかわいいとおもわない？
Don't you think dogs are cute?

Boy (frightened): そ…そうだね…
Sh... sure...

YOUNGER SISTER

妹

いもうと、マイ

ex. 妹さん (いもうとさん) - younger sister
ex. 義妹* (いもうと) - younger sister-in-law
ex. 妹分 (いもうとぶん) - protogee

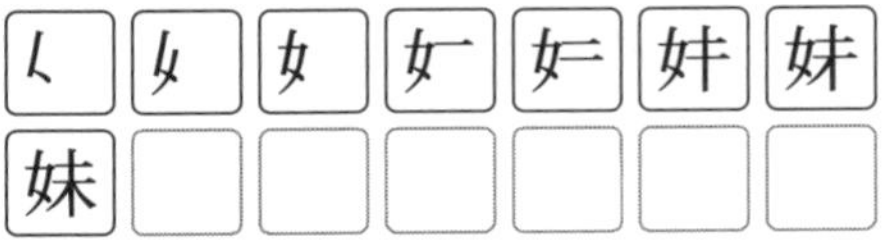

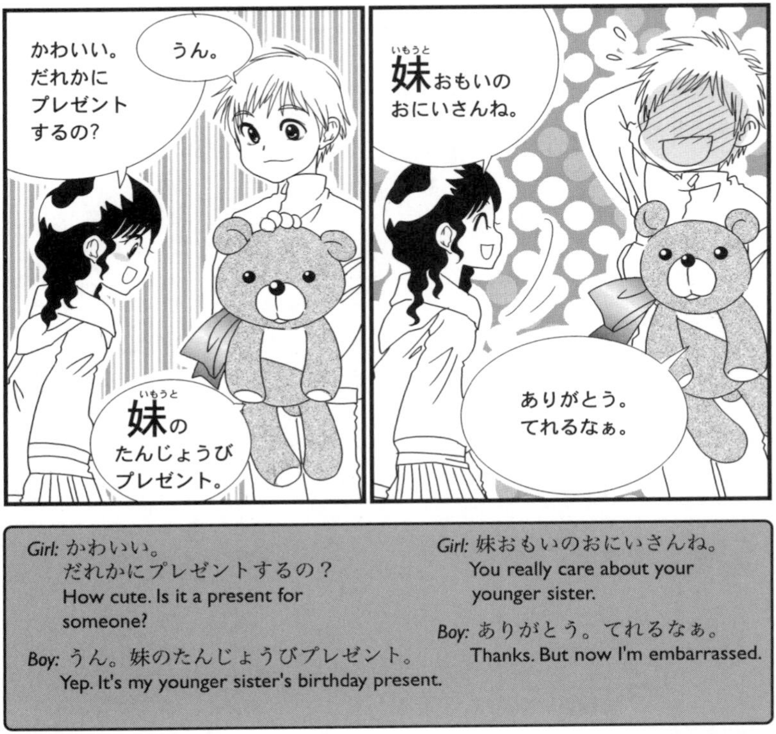
かわいい。だれかにプレゼントするの?
うん。
妹のたんじょうびプレゼント。
妹おもいのおにいさんね。
ありがとう。てれるなぁ。

Girl: かわいい。だれかにプレゼントするの？
How cute. Is it a present for someone?

Boy: うん。妹のたんじょうびプレゼント。
Yep. It's my younger sister's birthday present.

Girl: 妹おもいのおにいさんね。
You really care about your younger sister.

Boy: ありがとう。てれるなぁ。
Thanks. But now I'm embarrassed.

COLOR / PASSION

いろ、ショク、シキ

ex. 原色* (げんしょく) - primary colors
ex. 色彩* (しきさい) - hue; tint
ex. 顔色* (かおいろ) - complexion

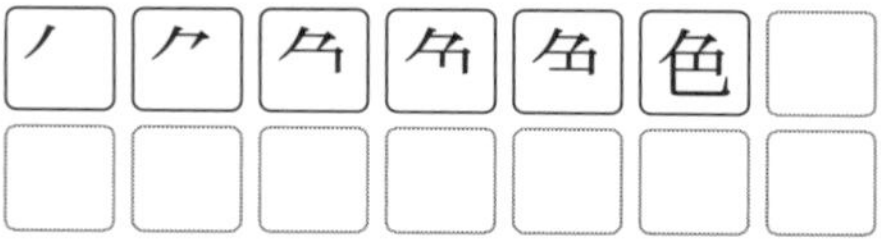

わぁ！
きれいな 色の
おかしが
たくさん！

色とりどり
だね。

どうしよう...
色いろあって
めうつりしちゃう〜。

Girl: わぁ！きれいな色の
おかしがたくさん！
Wow! There are so many
different-colored candies!

色とりどりだね。
A real variety of colors.

Girl: どうしよう...
色いろあって
めうつりしちゃう〜。
What should I do...
There are so many colors
to choose from.

FISH

うお、さかな、ギョ

ex. 金魚 (きんぎょ) - goldfish
ex. 魚座* (うおざ) - Pisces
ex. 人魚 (にんぎょ) - mermaid

魚

ねぇ、おじさんて
魚やさんでしょ?!
せいかい。
なんで
わかったんだい?
魚やだって。
魚や
おじさんが魚
みたいな
かおしているから!
ゲラゲラ
あははは
魚

Boy: ねぇ、おじさんて
魚やさんでしょ？！
Hey, mister, you work in a fish shop, don't you?!

Man: せいかい。なんで
わかったんだい？魚やだって。
That's right. How'd you know I worked in a fish shop?

Sign: 魚や (Fish Shop)

Boy: おじさんが魚みたいな
かおしているから！
Because your face looks like a fish!

ゲラゲラ (chuckling)
あははは (laughter)

CATTLE / COW

うし、ギュウ

ex. 牛肉 (ぎゅうにく) - beef
ex. 牛乳* (ぎゅうにゅう) - milk
ex. 子牛 (こうし) - calf

Boy: 牛がたくさんいるね。
There sure are a lot of cows.

ベロ
(sound of a tongue licking something)

Boy: (speechless)

SING / SONG

うた、うた(う)、カ

ex. 歌手 (かしゅ) - singer
ex. 歌を歌う (うたをうたう) - sing a song
ex. 国歌 (こっか) - national anthem

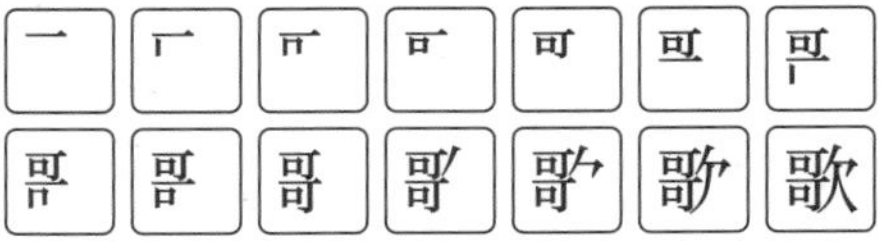

カラオケいこうよ!

え?!いいよ、
歌へただし。

ノリノリで歌ってるじゃない...
しかもじょうずだし...

Schoolgirl: カラオケ
　いこうよ!
　Let's go to a karaoke club!

Friend: え？！いいよ、歌へただし。
　Huh?! Forget it; I can't sing.

Classmates (thinking alike): ノリノリで歌ってる
じゃない...しかもじょうずだし...
Look who's talking... She's a great singer...

SEA / BEACH

うみ、カイ

ex. 海外 (かいがい) - overseas; foreign
ex. 海辺* (うみべ) - seashore
ex. 海草* (かいそう) - seaweed

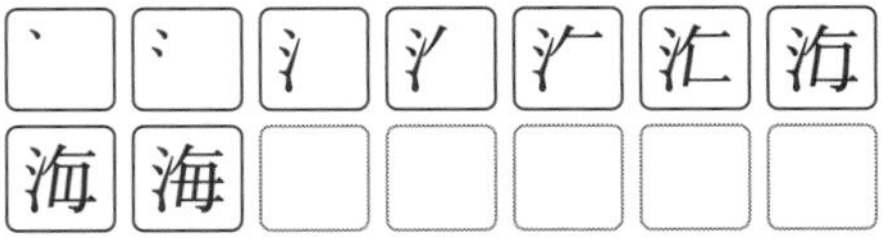

海

丶	冫	氵	汁	浐	浐	江	海
海	海						

なつといえば...

海だー!
海!
海!

Boy: なつといえば...	海だー!
Summer means...	海!
	海!
	The sea!
	Sea!
	Sea!

SELL

う(る)、う(れる)、バイ

ex. 売店 (ばいてん) - shop; vendor's stall
ex. 安売り* (やすうり) - discount sale
ex. 発売中* (はつばいちゅう) - now on sale

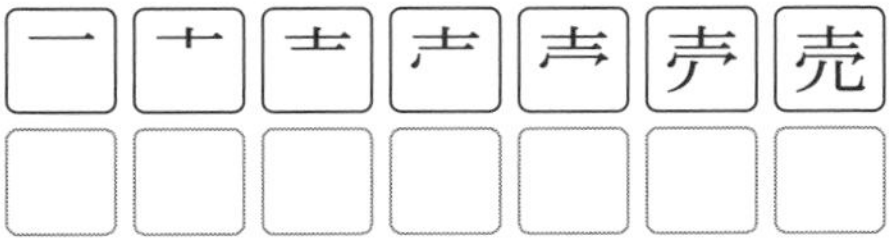

一 十 士 声 声 声 売

ものがいっぱい
だけど、いったい
どうしたの？

こんどの
フリーマーケットで
売りにだすものを
せいりしていたの。

たくさん
売れると
いいわね。

Big sister: ものがいっぱい だけど、
いったいどうしたの？
You sure have out a lot of stuff.
What's it for?

Little sister: こんどの フリーマーケットで
売りにだすものをせいりしていたの。
I'm looking for things to sell at the next
flea market.

Big sister: たくさん売れるといいわね。
I hope you're able to sell a lot.

MANY

おお(い)、タ

ex. 多すぎる (おおすぎる) - too much
ex. 多忙* (たぼう) - very busy
ex. 多分 (たぶん) - probably

| ノ | ク | タ | タ | 多 | 多 | |

Boy on left: このへんてひとが多いね。
There's a lot of people around here.

Boy on right: 多いね。
Definitely a lot.

SOUND

おと、ね、オン

ex. 音楽 (おんがく) - music
ex. 音声* (おんせい) - voice
ex. 騒音* (そうおん) - noise; cacophony

ヽ	亠	立	立	立	音
音	音				

音がくのじかん
ふえのテストだって!

れんしゅうしなくちゃ。

!!?

わあああ!
しっかりして!

Girl: 音がくのじかんふえのテストだって！
There's going to be a test during music class!

Boy: れんしゅうしなくちゃ。
We've gotta practice.

ばっ (sound of book being opened)

びっしり (sound of abundance;
the students are shocked when they
look at the sheet music and realize
how much they must practice)

ふらー (sound of fainting)

Girl: わあああ！しっかりして！
Hey! Get a grip!

YOUNGER BROTHER

おとうと、ダイ、テイ、デ

ex. 義弟* (おとうと) - younger brother-in-law
ex. 弟子 (でし) - disciple; apprentice
ex. 異父兄弟* (いふきょうだい) - half-brother

` 丷 丷 丷 弚 弟 弟

あれ？きみって
弟がいたんだ。

そうなの。
弟だってよく
わかったね。

ほら、
あいさつして。

こんにちは。

だって、
そっくりだもん。

こんにちは

Teen-age boy: あれ？きみって弟がいたんだ。
Huh? I didn't know you had a
younger brother.

Teen-age girl: そうなの。弟だってよく
わかったね。
That's right. But how'd you know
he's my brother?

Teen-age girl: ほら、あいさつして。
Say hello.

Little boy: こんにちは。Hello.

Teen-age boy: だって、
そっくりだもん。こんにちは...
You two look so alike. Hello...

SAME

おな(じ)、ドウ

ex. 同日 (どうじつ) - the same day
ex. 同志* (どうし) - kindrid spirit; soulmate
ex. 同様* (どうよう) - similar

| 一 | 冂 | 冂 | 同 | 同 | 同 | | |

きょうはどういう
かみがたに
しますか?

このげいのうじんと
同じかみがたで!
ファンなんです。

Beautician: きょうは
どういうかみがたに
しますか?
Have you decided
what kind of hairstyle
you want?

Customer: このげいのうじんと
同じかみがたで!
ファンなんです。
I want the same style as this
celebrity! I'm a big fan.

THINK

おも(う)、シ

ex. 思い出 (おもいで) - memories
ex. 不思議* (ふしぎ) - wonder; mystery
ex. 思想* (しそう) - thought; idea; ideology

丨	冂	冂	田	田	田	思
思	思					

なつかしいな。

わぁ...

アルバム
だぁ。

いろいろな
思いでが
つまっていて...

じぶんの
たからもの
だと
思うわ。

Young woman: なつかしいな。
わぁ...
How nostalgic. Wow...

アルバムだぁ。
My photo album.

いろいろな思いでが
つまっていて...
It's full of so many good memories.

じぶんのたからもの
だと思うわ。
I think of it as my treasure.

PICTURE

ガ、カク

ex. 画家 (がか) - artist; painter
ex. 漫画* (まんが) - manga (cartoon; comic)
ex. 映画* (えいが) - movie

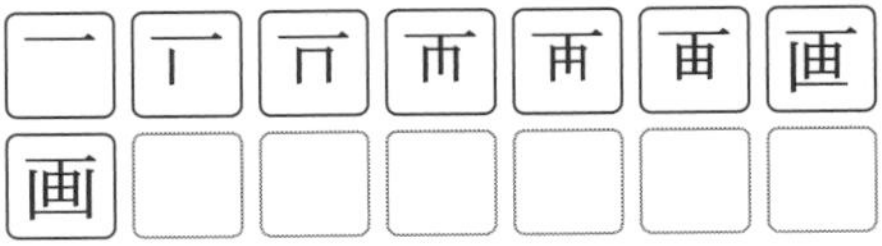

画

かい画てんじかい
さすが画はく!
画はく ひとこと。
なんちゃって…

Sign: かい画てんじかい (Art Exhibition)

Visitor: さすが画はく！
You're a wonderful painter!

News reporter: 画はくひとこと。
Please tell us about your picture.

Boy (daydreaming):
なんちゃって…
Woudn't that be great...

BUY

か(う)、バイ

ex. 買い主* (かいぬし) - buyer
ex. 買い物* (かいもの) - shopping
ex. 買収* (ばいしゅう) - bribery

きょうは、
スーパーやすうりの
ひだわ！

お買いどく
ひんばかり！

すぐ買いにいかなくちゃ！

セール↓
かいじょう

Housewife: きょうは、
　　　　　　スーパーやすうりの
　　　　　　ひだわ！
There's a special sale at the
supermarket today!

お買いどくひんばかり！
Lots of good buys!

すぐ買いにいかなくちゃ！
I've gotta get there early to shop!

Sign: セールかいじょう (Sales Floor)

RETURN

ex. 帰宅* (きたく) - returning home
ex. 帰国 (きこく) - returning to one's country
ex. 帰り道 (かえりみち) - the way back home

帰

ただいまー!

おかえり。
...ちょっと!
ちょっとまちなさい!

ドタドタ

帰ったらくつくらい
そろえなさい。
おやつぬきに
するからね!

......

......

いそいそ

Boy (running): ただいまー!I'm home!
ドタドタ (sound of boy running up the stairs)
Mother: おかえり。...ちょっと!ちょっとまちなさい!
　Hi. ...Hey! Hey, wait!
　帰ったらくつくらいそろえなさい。
　おやつぬきにするからね!
　Put your shoes away when you return home
　or there will be no snacks for you!

Mother: (speechless)

Boy: (speechless)

いそいそ (sound of
shoes being dragged
across the floor)

WIND

かぜ、かざ、フウ

ex. 台風 (たいふう) - typhoon
ex. 風邪* (かぜ) - cold (illness)
ex. 風変わり* (ふうがわり) - strange

丿	几	凡	凡	同	同	風
風	風					

こんにちは。

?!!

風がわりな
かみがたして
なにかあった？

そと、風がつよくて
こんなになっちゃった。

ビュー

おつかれ。

Wife: こんにちは。
　　　Hey.

Husband: 風がわりなかみがた
　　　してなにかあった？
　　　What's with the strange hairstyle?

Wife: そと、風がつよくて
　　　こんなになっちゃった。
　　　The strong wind did this.

ビュー (sound of a wind gust)

Husband: おつかれ。
　　　Poor you.

WAY OF DOING

かた、ホウ

ex. 作り方 (つくりかた) - the way to make
ex. 方言 (ほうげん) - dialect
ex. 正方形* (せいほうけい) - square

方

どうしたの？
こまっているみたい。

じつは、
すうがくの
もんだいで、

とき方がわからない
もんだいがあるんだ。

あぁ、
このもんだいは
したのこうしきを
つかった
方がいいよ。

ありがとう。
これなら
とけそうだよ。

Big brother: どうしたの？
こまっているみたい。
What's wrong? You look like
you could use some help.

Little brother: じつは、すうがくの
もんだいで、とき方がわからない
もんだいがあるんだ。
I don't know how to do this math problem.

Big brother: あぁ、このもんだいはしたの
こうしきをつかった方がいいよ。
Ah, with this type of problem, it's best
to do it the way that's written here.

Little brother: ありがとう。これならとけ
そうだよ。
Thanks. I think I can solve it now.

紙

PAPER

かみ、シ

ex. 折り紙* (おりがみ) - origami
ex. 紙袋* (かみぶくろ) - paper bag
ex. 包装紙* (ほうそうし) - wrapping paper

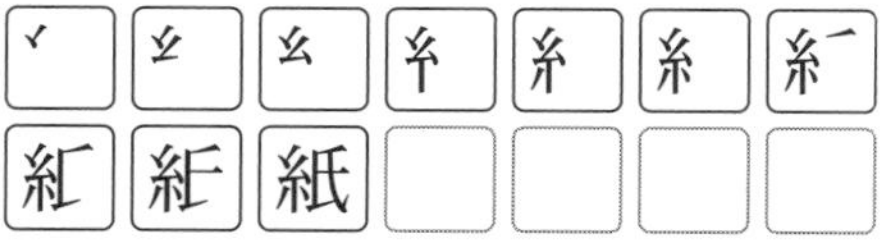

だい5かい
がみ
おり紙てん
てんじみてみない?
いいよ。
がみ
すべており紙でできているなんてしんじられない!
がみ
おり紙ってすごいのね。しらなかったわ。

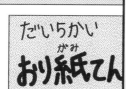

Sign: だい５かい
おり紙てん
(5th Origami Exhibition)

First girl: てんじみてみない？
You want to check out the exhibition?

Second girl: いいよ。 Sure.

First girl: すべており紙で
できているなんてしんじられない！
I can't believe all the things that are made with origami!

Second girl: おり紙ってすごいのね。
しらなかったわ。
Origami really is amazing. I never knew.

THINK

かんが(える)、コウ

ex. 考え事* (かんがえごと) - deep thinking
ex. 考査* (こうさ) - examination; test
ex. 考案* (こうあん) - idea; plan

一　十　土　耂　耂　考

考えても
考えても
ぜんぜん
わから
ないよ!

Schoolboy: うーん	考えても
Hmm...	考えても
	ぜんぜんわからないよ!
うーんと…	I think...
Uhhh...	and I think...
	and still I can't understand any of this!

CAPITAL

キョウ、ケイ

ex. 東京 (とうきょう) - Tokyo
ex. 京都* (きょうと) - Kyoto
ex. 北京 (ぺきん) - Beijing

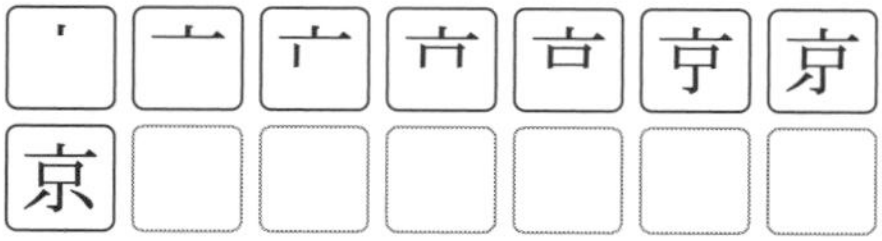

じょう**京**して
はや3ねん...

よし!

ビシッ

スーツきるのも
さまになって
きたかな。

College student: じょう京してはや3ねん...
   It's been 3 years since I've been
   to the capital city...

よし！
All right!

ビシッ ("sound" of looking good)

スーツきるのも
さまになってきたかな。
I feel like I finally belong in
this suit!

CUT

切

きる、きっ、セツ、サイ

ex. 大切 (たいせつ) - important; valuable
ex. 切手 (きって) - postage stamp
ex. 切符* (きっぷ) - ticket

一	七	切	切			

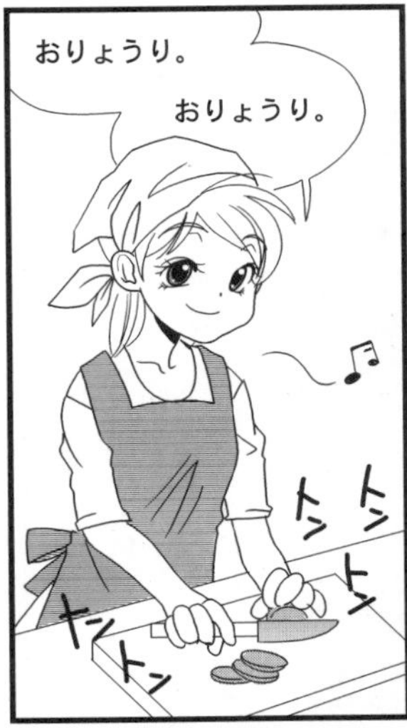

おりょうり。
おりょうり。
トン
トン
トン
トン

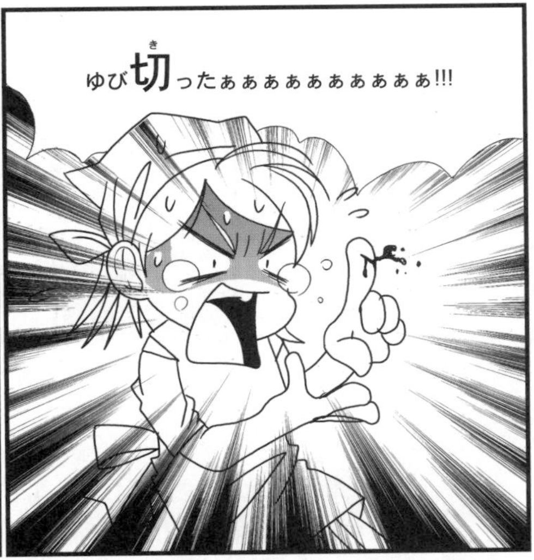

ゆび切ったぁぁぁぁぁぁぁぁぁぁ!!!

Housewife (singing to herself):
おりょうり。おりょうり。
Cooking. Cooking.

トントントントントントン
(chopping sound)

ゆび切ったぁぁぁぁぁぁぁぁぁぁ！
I cut my fingerrrrrrrrrrrr!

MOUTH

くち、コウ、ク

ex. 口拭き* (くちふき) - napkin
ex. 口づけ (くちづけ) - kiss
ex. 口笛* (くちぶえ) - whistle

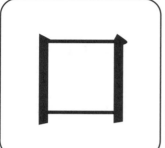

さっき、

ごはん
たべた？

なっ、
なんで
そんなこと
わかるの？

だって、

口
くち
のまわりに
ごはんがついてるから。

Sister: さっき、ごはん
たべた？
Did you just finish eating?

Brother: なっ、なんでそんな
ことわかるの？
Yeah, how did you know?

Sister: だって、口のまわりに
ごはんがついてるから。
Because you've got rice stuck
around your mouth.

BLACK

くろ、くろ(い)、コク

ex. 黒猫* (くろねこ) - black cat
ex. 黒人 (こくじん) - black person
ex. 黒帯* (くろおび) - black belt (martial arts)

黒

!!!
つるっ
!!
ズザザザザドスン
......
けほ。
わわっ!
まっ黒(くろ)
サンタクロースだ!

つるっ
(slipping sound)

ズザザザザドスン
(tumbling sound)

Santa: (speechless)

けほ (exhale)

Boy: わわっ！まっ黒サンタクロースだ！
Yikes! Santa is pitch-black!

工

MANUFACTURE

コウ、ク

ex. 工事* (こうじ) - construction work
ex. 工場* (こうじょう) - factory
ex. 人工 (じんこう) - man-made

一	丅	工				

こう
工じょうがたくさんあるとくうきがわるいね。
うん。

First boy: 工じょうがたくさんあると くうきがわるいね。
All of these factories sure make the air bad around here.

Second boy: うん。
Yup.

HEART / SPIRIT

こころ、シン

ex. 心細い* (こころぼそい) - lonely
ex. 心音 (しんおん) - heartbeat (sound of)
ex. 心残り* (こころのこり) - regret

'	心	心	心				

あしたから
みなみのしまに
りょこう...

ほわん

ほわん

こころ
心が
はずむわぁ。

こころ
心ここにあらずだな...

Sister: あしたからみなみのしまに
りょこう...
Tomorrow we begin vacationing
on a southern island...

ほわんほわん (happiness in the heart)

心がはずむわぁ。
My heart is beating with excitement.

Brother: 心ここにあらずだな...
Her heart is already in another place...

ANSWER / REPLY

こた(え)、こた(える)、トウ

ex. 答える (こたえる) - to reply
ex. 答案用紙* (とうあんようし) - exam paper
ex. 解答* (かいとう) - answer; solution

ノ	⺊	⺅	⺮	⺮	⺮	竺
笂	笒	笭	答	答		

このもんだいの
答えがわかるひとは
いるかな?

Q1.

はーい

Teacher: このもんだいの答えがわかるひとはいるかな?
Does anyone know the answer to the question?

Students (in unison): はーい
Ye-esssss!

CHARACTER

ジ

字

ex. 漢字* (かんじ) - kanji
ex. 字画 (じかく) - kanji stroke count
ex. 字体* (じたい) - font; lettering

うわっ。
きたない
字(じ)だな。
なんてかいてあるのか
まったく
よめないよ…

Schoolboy: うわっ。
きたない字だな。
Wow. What messy writing.

なんてかいてあるのか
まったくよめないよ…
I can't read this at all...

週

WEEK

シュウ

ex. 先週 (せんしゅう) - last week
ex. 今週 (こんしゅう) - this week
ex. 週末* (しゅうまつ) - weekend

あしたは
げつようび…
1週かんってたつのが
はやいなぁ。
しみじみ…
はやく
ねなさい。
もう、
おそい
わよ。
SUN. MO
キュッ

キュッ (sound of pencil on paper)	*Boy:* あしたはげつようび… 1週かんってたつのがはやいなぁ。 Tomorrow's Monday...The week sure goes by quickly. しみじみ (sound of confidence) *Mother:* はやくねなさい。もう、おそいわよ。 Hurry up and go to bed. It's already late.

KNOW

し(る)、チ

ex. 知能* (ちのう) - intelligence
ex. 知人 (ちじん) - acquaintance
ex. 知識* (ちしき) - knowledge

このかんじの
よみかた **知**ってる?

ああ、
これは
こう。

こっちの
よみかた。

これは?

あと
これ。

これは
こう。

すごくかんじのよみかた
知ってるんだね。

さすが。

いやぁ、
てれるよ。

Teacher: このかんじの
よみかた知ってる?
Do you know how
to read this kanji?

Student: ああ、
これはこう。
Ah, like this.

Teacher: これは？
This one?
Student: こっちのよみかた。
It's read like this.
Teacher: あとこれ。
And this?
Student: これはこう。
This way.

Teacher: すごくかんじの
よみかた知ってるんだね。
いやぁ、てれるよ。
You know how to read a lot
of kanji. I'm impressed.

Student: さすが。
It's nothing.

少

LITTLE

すく(ない)、すこ(し)、ショウ

ex. 少しずつ (すこしずつ) - little by little
ex. 少女 (しょうじょ) - little (young) girl
ex. 少年 (しょうねん) - little (young) boy

亅	小	小	少			

ふー…
あと少(すこ)しで…
しゅくだいがおわりそう!

Schoolboy: ふー…
Whew...

あと少しで…
Just a little more...

しゅくだいがおわりそう！
And my homework will be done!

SKY / AIR / EMPTY

そら、あ(く)、あ(ける)、から、クウ

ex. 空色 (そらいろ) - sky-blue
ex. 空港* (くうこう) - airport
ex. 空手 (からて) - karate (empty hands)

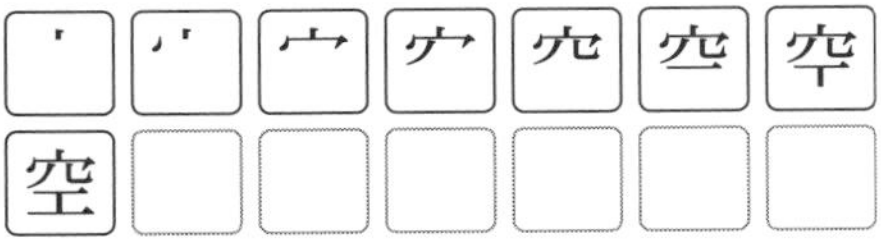

空

空(そら)はあおくてきれいだし。
空(くう)きはおいしいし。
しぜんってさいこうだなぁ。

Boy: 空はあおくてきれいだし。
The sky is so blue and beautiful.

空きはおいしいし。
The air smells so fresh.

しぜんって
さいこうだなぁ。
Nature is wonderful.

RICE FIELD

た、デン

ex. 田んぼ (たんぼ) - farmland; rice paddy
ex. 田植え* (たうえ) - rice planting
ex. 田園* (でんえん) - rural area

丨	冂	田	田	田		

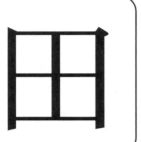

田んぼに
おたま
じゃくし。

たくさん。

おとうさんがこどものころは
このへんは田んぼだらけ
だったんだよ。

そうなんだ。

へぇー

Father: 田んぼにおたまじゃくし。
There are tadpoles in this
paddy field.

Son: たくさん。
Lots of 'em.

Father: おとうさんがこどものころは
このへんは田んぼだらけだったんだよ。
When daddy was your age, there were
a lot more rice paddies around here.

Daughter: そうなんだ。Is that so?

Son: へぇー Really?

STAND / TABLE

ダイ、タイ

台

ex. 台紙 (だいし) - cardboard
ex. 台所* (だいどころ) - kitchen
ex. 台湾* (たいわん) - Taiwan

あと
もうすこし…
なにか
台になるもの
ないかなぁ。
台に
なるもの。

Girl (reaching): あと
もうすこし…
Just a bit more...

なにか台になるものないかなぁ。
I wonder if there's a stand I can use.

台になるもの。
Something like a stool.

CORRECT

ただ(しい)、ただ(す)、セイ、ショウ

ex. 正解* (せいかい) - correct answer
ex. 正誤* (せいご) - correction
ex. 正月 (しょうがつ) - New Year

もんだいです。

正しいものは
どれでしょう?

いち!

正かい!

Teacher: もんだいです。
Here's the question.

正しいものは
どれでしょう?
Which is the correct
answer?

Student: いち！
Number one!

Teacher: 正かい！
Correct!

STAND

た(つ)、た(てる)、リツ

立

ex. 立ち席* (たちせき) - standing room only
ex. 立て前 (たてまえ) - official position; stance
ex. 立食 (りっしょく) - buffet (stand-up meal)

ずっと、せいざして
いたら、あしが
しびれて
立てない…
へいき?
ぢん
ぢん
ぎゃぁぁぁぁぁぁぁ!
つん
しびれて
いるから
さわらないで!

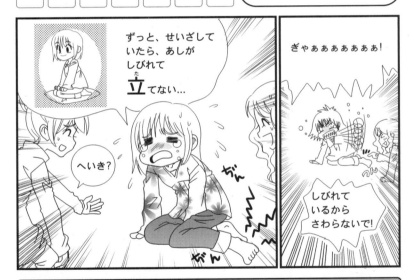

Girl in center: ずっと、せいざして
いたら、あしがしびれて立てない…
My legs fell asleep because I was sitting Japanese-style, and now I can't stand up!

Girl on left: へいき？
Are you OK?

ぢんぢん (sound of numbness)

Girl in center:
ぎゃぁぁぁぁぁぁぁ！
Aaarrrggghhh!

つん (poke)

しびれているから
さわらないで！
Don't touch, they're asleep!

PLEASURE / MUSIC

たの(しい)、たの(しむ)、ガク、ラク

ex. 楽しみ (たのしみ) - enjoyment
ex. 音楽 (おんがく) - music
ex. 楽ちん (らくちん) - easy-going

ヨロヨロヨロ
(sound of difficult pedaling uphill)

Cyclist: 楽ちん！楽ちん！
Easy! Easy!

シャアアアアアア...
(sound of bike zooming downhill)

楽しい！
Fun!

GROUND

地

チ、ジ

ex. 地下 (ちか) - underground
ex. 地震* (じしん) - earthquake
ex. 地元 (じもと) - local

一	十	土	圠	地	地	

うわぁぁぁ!
ぐら
ぐら
ぐら
地しんだ!
ぐらぐら…
すごい ゆれだ!
地しんだ!
あそんでー!
ゆっさ
ゆっさ
おきて!
うー
ん…

Brother: うわぁぁぁ！
Ahhh!

ぐらぐらぐら (rumble)

地しんだ！
Earthquake!

Brother (dreaming): 地しんだ！すごいゆれだ！
Earthquake! The Big One!

Sister: あそんでー！おきて!
Let's play! Wake up!

ゆっさゆっさ (sound of girl shaking brother)

Brother (awake): うーん… Sh-sure...

NEAR / CLOSE BY

ちか(い)、キン

ex. 近道 (ちかみち) - shortcut
ex. 近年 (きんねん) - recent years
ex. 近所* (きんじょ) - neighborhood

一	厂	斤	斤	沂	近	近

パンダのあかちゃんて
ぬいぐるみみたいで
かわいい!
こんな近くで
みたの
はじめて。

近くて
ラッキー!

Girl on left: パンダのあかちゃんてぬいぐるみ
みたいでかわいい!
こんな近くでみたのはじめて。
Baby pandas are so cute, they look just like
stuffed toys! I've never seen one up close before.

Girl on right: 近くてラッキー!
We sure are lucky to get so close!

STRENGTH / POWER

ちから、リョク、リキ

ex. 気力 (きりょく) - energy; vitality
ex. 電力 (でんりょく) - electric power
ex. 力持ち* (ちからもち) - muscleman

㇆ 力

力

ふぬぬぬ…
ぐ…
ビンのフタが あかない!
ちから
力まかせに あけても だめよ。
コツさえつかめば、
ちから
力なんてひつよう ないかもよ。
!!
ぱかっ

Boy: ふぬぬぬ…
ぐ…
(grunting noises)

ビンのフタが
あかない！
I can't get this lid off!

Mother: 力まかせに
あけてもだめよ。
Sometimes strength isn't the solution.

Mother: コツさえつかめば、
力なんてひつようない
かもよ。
If you know how to do it, you don't need to use much force at all.

ぱかっ (pop)

茶

TEA

チャ、サ

ex. 茶店 (さてん) - teahouse
ex. 茶色 (ちゃいろ) - brown
ex. 茶道* (さどう) - tea ceremony

シャカ
シャカ
シャカ
カコーーン
お茶(ちゃ)かいって
たのしいわね?
ほんとう。
おまっ茶(ちゃ)も
おいしいわ。

シャカシャカシャカ
(shaking noise)

カコーン
(pouring noise)

Woman in kimono: お茶かいってたのしいわね?
Tea ceremony get-togethers sure are fun, aren't they?

Second woman: ほんとう。おまっ茶もおいしいわ。
They sure are. And macha* tea is delicious.

*Macha is a frothy green tea used in traditional tea-pouring ceremonies.

MAKE / CREATE

作

つく(る)、サク、サ

ex. 工作室 (こうさくしつ) - workshop
ex. 手作り (てづくり) - handmade
ex. 作家* (さっか) - author; novelist

みなさん、しゅくだいの
作(さく)ぶんは かいて きましたか?
はーい!!
けんじくん よんでみて。
はい。
「はじめて作(つく)った プラモデル」

Teacher: みなさん、しゅくだいの作ぶんはかいてきましたか？
Has everyone finished writing the essays I assigned for homework?

Students (in unison): はーい！！
Ye-esss!

Teacher: けんじくんよんでみて。
Kenji, you read yours first.

Kenji: はい。
「はじめて作ったプラモデル」
OK.
"The first plastic model I ever made."

(The symbols 「 」 are used as quotation marks in Japanese.)

強

STRONG

つよ(い)、つよ(まる)、キョウ、ゴウ

ex. 強大 (きょうだい) - mighty; powerful
ex. 強力 (ごうりき) - enormous strength
ex. 強引* (ごういん) - overbearing

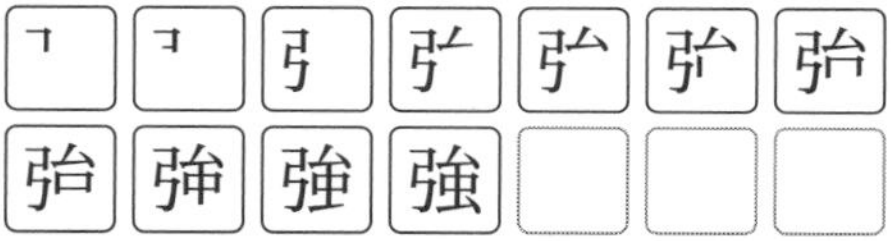

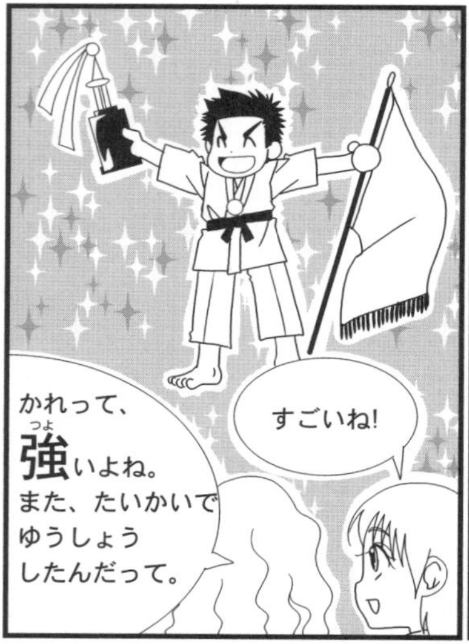
かれって、強いよね。また、たいかいでゆうしょうしたんだって。
すごいね!

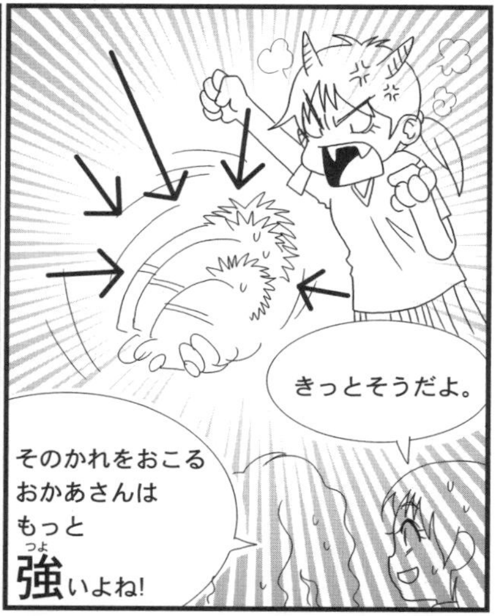
そのかれをおこるおかあさんはもっと強いよね!
きっとそうだよ。

Girl on left: かれって強いよね。また、たいかいでゆうしょうしたんだって。
He sure is strong. He won the tourmanent again.

Girl on right: すごいね!
Incredible!

Girl on left: そのかれをおこるおかあさんはもっと強いよね!
But I'll bet the mother who scolds him is even stronger!

Girl on right: きっとそうだよ。
My thoughts exactly.

HAND

て、シュ

ex. 手袋* (てぶくろ) - glove
ex. 手書き (てがき) - hand-drawn
ex. 握手* (あくしゅ) - handshake

一 二 三 手

手

ぇぇぇ?!これぜんぶ
手づくり?!
手づくりって、
プロなみよ!
がしっ
こんなに
ごつい…
おおきな
手なのに。
ありがとう。
てれ
てれ
てれ
すごいよ!
すご
すぎ
だよ!

Girl (looking at handicrafts): ぇぇぇ？！
これぜんぶ手づくり？！
What?! All these things are handmade?!

手づくりって、
プロなみよ！
Handmade, just like a pro!

がしっ (sound of holding a hand)

Girl: こんなにごつい…おおきな手なのに。
By this rough and large hand...
すごいよ！すごすぎだよ！
Cool! Really cool!

Craftsman: ありがとう。Thanks.

てれてれてれ (sound of embarrassment)

止

STOP

と(まる)、と(める)、シ

ex. 止まれ (とまれ) - stop (traffic) sign
ex. 禁止* (きんし) - prohibition; ban
ex. 中止 (ちゅうし) - suspension

わっ
ぎゃっ
!
びっくりしたー… しんぞう 止(と)まるかと おもったよぉ!
ごめんね。

Boy: わっ
Boo!
Girl: ぎゃっ!
Eeek!

Girl: びっくりしたー…しんぞう止まるかと おもったよぉ!
You nearly scared me to death… I thought my heart had stopped!

Boy: ごめんね。
Sorry.

BIRD

とり、チョウ

ex. 野鳥 (やちょう) - wild bird
ex. 鳥肌* (とりはだ) - goosebumps
ex. 焼き鳥* (やきとり) - grilled chicken

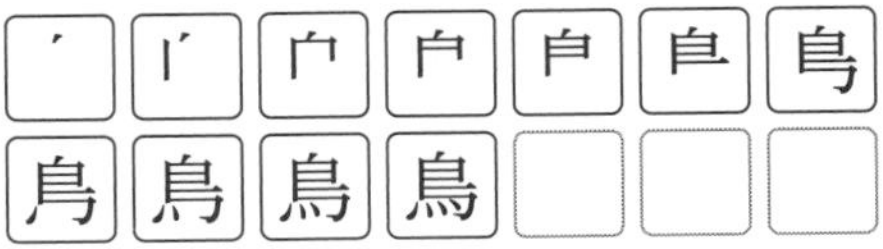

鳥

鳥ってすべて とべるのかしら?
とべない 鳥もいるよ。
ダチョウ とか ペンギンは とべない 鳥だね。
なるほど。

Girl: 鳥ってすべて
とべるのかしら？
Can all birds fly?

Boy: とべない鳥もいるよ。
There are some birds that can't.

Boy: ダチョウとかペンギンは
とべない鳥だね。
Birds such as the ostrich and the penguin can't fly.

Girl: なるほど。
Gotcha.

夏

SUMMER

なつ、カ、ゲ

ex. 夏休み (なつやすみ) - summer vacation
ex. 夏時間 (なつじかん) - summertime
ex. 夏至* (げし) - summer solstice

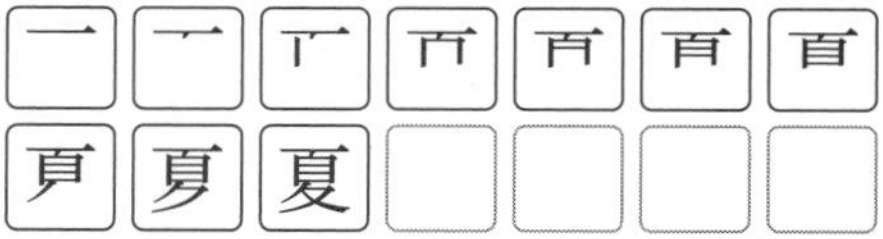

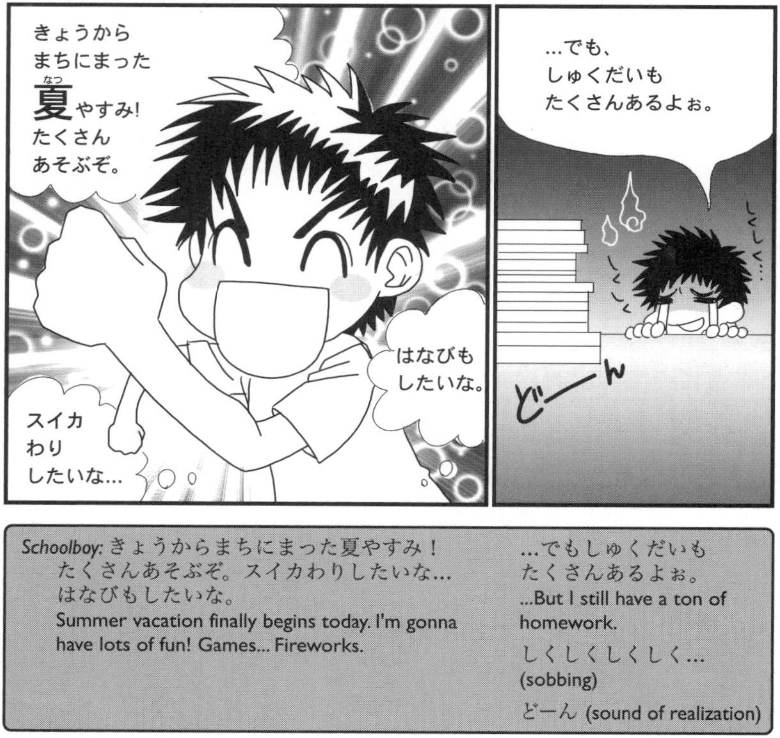
きょうから
まちにまった
夏やすみ!
たくさん
あそぶぞ。
はなびも
したいな。
スイカ
わり
したいな…
…でも、
しゅくだいも
たくさんあるよぉ。
しくしく…
しくしく
どーん

Schoolboy: きょうからまちにまった夏やすみ！たくさんあそぶぞ。スイカわりしたいな…はなびもしたいな。
Summer vacation finally begins today. I'm gonna have lots of fun! Games... Fireworks.

…でもしゅくだいもたくさんあるよぉ。
...But I still have a ton of homework.

しくしくしくしく…
(sobbing)

どーん (sound of realization)

MEAT / FLESH

ニク

ex. 肉親* (にくしん) - blood relative
ex. 肉球* (にくきゅう) - animal paw
ex. 筋肉* (きんにく) - muscle

丨	冂	内	内	肉	肉	

肉

にく
肉きゅう
きもちいい!
ぷにぷに
してる～!

にく
きみの肉きゅうは
ぷにぷにしていて
きもちいいね。
いいめいわく
なんだって。
やみつきに
なりそう。

Girl: 肉きゅうきもちいい！
ぷにぷにしてる～！
Your paws feel so good!
So squishy!

Girl: きみの肉きゅうはぷにぷにしていて
きもちいいね。やみつきになりそう。
Your paws are soooo squishy and comfortable.
I can't stop feeling them.

Cat: いいめいわくなんだって。
You're really starting to get on my nerves.

FIELD

の、ヤ

ex. 野天 (のてん) - in the open; the open air
ex. 野性* (やせい) - wild (nature)
ex. 野宿* (のじゅく) - camping

| l | 冂 | 日 | 日 | 甲 | 甲 | 里 |
| 野 | 野 | 野 | 野 | | | |

テントの
じゅんびはできたね。

きょうはここで
野じゅくだね。

あ、そうそう。

野せい
どうぶつには

じゅうぶん
きをつけてね。

ドドドドドド

あ…

Boy: テントのじゅんび
はできたね。
You put the tent up.

Girl: きょうはここで
野じゅくだね。
We'll camp out
here today.

Girl: あ、そうそう。
野せいどうぶつには
じゅうぶんきをつけてね。
Oh, by the way, watch out
for wild animals.

ドドドドドドド
(sound of fast running)

Girl: あ… Whoa!

RUN

走

はし(る)、ソウ

ex. 走者* (そうしゃ) - runner
ex. 競走* (きょうそう) - race
ex. 走塁* (そうるい) - base running (baseball)

一	十	土	𰀁	𰀁	𰀁	走

ドタ
バタ
ドタ
ドタ
!
ろうかは走らない!あぶないだろう!きをつけなさい!
ろうかは走らない
あぶないだろ!!!
ぴたっ
ぴたっ

ドタバタドタドタ
(sound of running)

Teacher: (surprised)

Teacher: ろうかは走らない！あぶないだろう！きをつけなさい！
No running in the hallway! It's dangerous! Be careful!

Sign: ろうかは走らない (No Running In The Hallway)

ぴたっぴたっ (sound of slower running)

FLOWER

はな、カ

ex. 生け花 (いけばな) - flower arrangement
ex. 花見 (はなみ) - blossom-viewing
ex. 花火 (はなび) - fireworks

Little girl: いちめんお花ばたけだわ！
It's a carpet of flowers!

EARLY / QUICK

はや(い)、はや(まる)、はや(める)、ソウ

ex. 早出 (はやで) - early arrival
ex. 早朝 (そうちょう) - early morning
ex. 早口 (はやくち) - fast talking

丨	冂	刀	日	旦	早	

早おきするぞ!

もう
こんな
じかん。

!!!

いそが
なきゃ。

早くもちこくしそう!

たいへんだ。
バスがいっちゃうよ。

Businessman:
早おきするぞ！
I'm gonna get up early
tomorrow.

もうこんなじかん。
It's already *what* time?

いそがなきゃ。
I've gotta hurry.

早くもちこくしそう！
たいへんだ。
バスがいっちゃうよ。
I'm already late!
This is terrible.
I'm gonna miss my bus.

SPRING

はる、シュン

ex. 春風 (しゅんぷう) - spring breeze
ex. 春巻き* (はるまき) - spring roll
ex. 青春 (せいしゅん) - youth

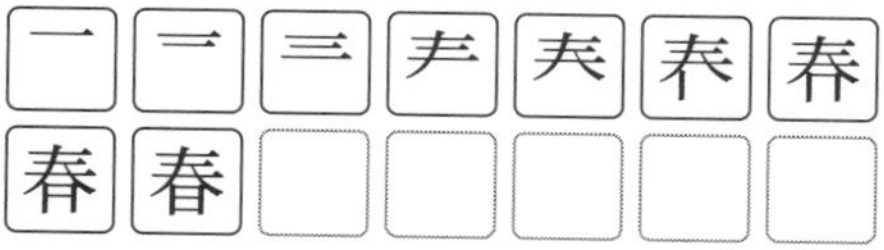

| 一 | 二 | 三 | 丰 | 夫 | 表 | 春 |
| 春 | 春 | | | | | |

きせつさきどりで
春コート
かっちゃった!

春まで
まてない
もの。

で...でも、
さきどりしすぎた
みたい...さむいよ。

ガチガチ

ガチ

春はまだ?

Schoolgirl: きせつさきどりで春コート
かっちゃった！
I got a head start and bought a new
spring coat!

春までまてないもの。
I just couldn't wait till spring.

で...でも、さきどりしすぎた
みたい...さむいよ。
B...but, I think I jumped the gun.
It's cold out.

ガチガチガチ (shivering)

春はまだ？ Is it spring yet?

DAYTIME / NOON

昼

ひる、チュウ

ex. 昼間 (ひるま) - daytime
ex. 昼休み (ひるやすみ) - lunchtime
ex. 昼寝* (ひるね) - nap

きょうの昼（ひる）ごはんは
なんにしようかな…
まようなぁ。
うーん。
ラーメン、
いや、
セットも…
トン
トン
はやくしないと
昼（ひる）やすみ
おわっちゃうよ。
!!

Schoolboy: きょうの昼ごはんはなんにしようかな…
I wonder what I should have for lunch today...

まようなぁ。うーん。ラーメン、いや、セットも…
I can't decide. Hmmm. Ramen, nah, or maybe a lunch set...

トントン (finger-tapping)

Schoolgirl: はやくしないと昼やすみおわっちゃうよ。
You better hurry or lunchtime will be over.

WIDE

ひろ(い)、ひろ(げる)、コウ

ex. 広大 (こうだい) - huge
ex. 広間 (ひろま) - large room; hall
ex. 広場* (ひろば) - plaza

うわー...
広いへやだね。

Boy: うわー... 広いへやだね。
Wow... It sure is a wide room.

WINTER

ふゆ、トウ

ex. 冬休み (ふゆやすみ) - winter vacation
ex. 冬眠* (とうみん) - hibernation
ex. 冬至* (とうじ) - winter solstice

ノ　ク　夂　冬　冬

冬って

いろいろ
イベントもあって
たのしいけど...

さむいから
くまみたいに
冬みんしたいなぁ。

いいから、
おきな
さい。

Little boy: 冬っていろいろ
イベントもあって
たのしいけど...
There are lots of fun events
to go to during the winter...

Little boy: さむいからくまみたいに
冬みんしたいなぁ。
But it's so cold I just want to hibernate
like a bear.

Big sister: いいから、おきなさい。
Come on, outta bed.

古

OLD

ふる(い)、ふる(す)、コ

ex. 古風 (こふう) - old customs
ex. 古物* (こぶつ) - antique
ex. 古寺* (ふるでら) - old temple

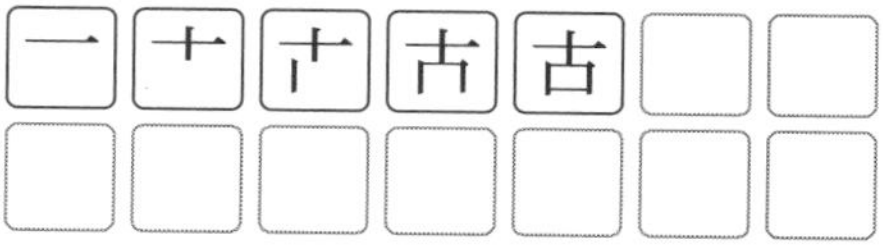

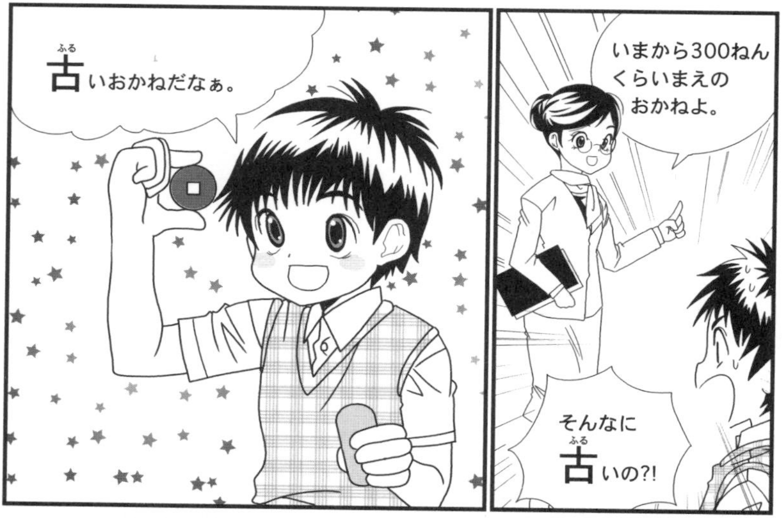

古(ふる)いおかねだなぁ。
いまから300ねん くらいまえの おかねよ。
そんなに 古(ふる)いの?!

Boy: 古いおかねだなぁ。
Hey, it's an old coin.

Teacher: いまから300ねん
くらいまえの
おかねよ。
It's actually about
300 years old.

Boy: そんなに古いの？！
It's that old?!

LETTER / WRITINGS

ブン、モン

ex. 文章* (ぶんしょう) - sentence
ex. 文字 (もじ) - letter (of alphabet); character
ex. 文化* (ぶんか) - culture; civilization

うーん...
文しょうもんだいって
にがてだなぁ。

文しょうもんだいで
なくてもにがて
だけど...

トホホ...

Boy: うーん...
文しょうもんだいってにがてだなぁ。
Ugh...
I don't like long-sentence homework problems.

文しょうもんだいで
なくてもにがてだけど...
Then again, I don't like the short-sentence ones either...

トホホ...
Sigh...

ENDEAVOR

ベン

ex. 勉強 (べんきょう) - study
ex. 勉学 (べんがく) - pursuit of knowledge
ex. 勉強家 (べんきょうか) - diligent student

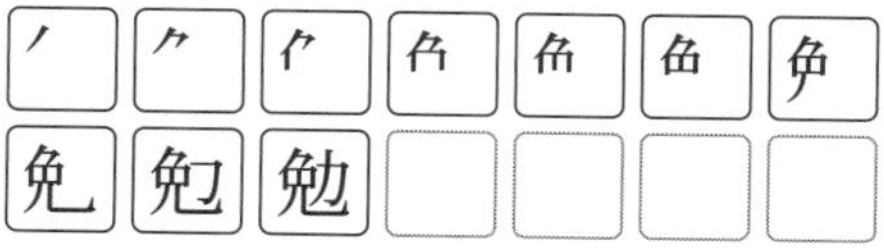

ノ	ク	广	夕	鱼	鱼	角
免	知	勉				

けんじくんて勉きょうねっしんね。

がくせいたるもの勉きょうがほんぎょうだとおもっていますから。

おぉ。

ぱち ぱち

ぱち

Schoolgirl: けんじくんて勉きょう
ねっしんね。
Kenji, you really enjoy
studying, don't you?

Kenji: がくせいたるもの
勉きょうがほんぎょう
だとおもっていますから。
As a student, I believe it's our
duty to study.

Schoolgirl: おぉ。Yeah.
ぱちぱちぱち (clapping)

TOWN

町

まち、チョウ

ex. 町会 (ちょうかい) - town council

ex. 町民* (ちょうみん) - townspeople

ex. 町外れ (まちはずれ) - outskirts of town

はなやみどりがたくさんあってすてき。
とてもいい町ね。
町ぜんたいで
とりくんでいるんだ。
そうなんだ…

Girl: はなやみどりがたくさんあってすてき。とてもいい町ね。
All these flowers and plants make it so beautiful. This is such a nice city.

Boy: 町ぜんたいでとりくんでいるんだ。
The entire city works together to keep it looking this way.

Girl: そうなんだ…
You don't say...

店

SHOP / STORE

みせ、テン

ex. 本店 (ほんてん) - main store; head office
ex. 店員* (てんいん) - store clerk
ex. 店先 (みせさき) - storefront

すてき!
これぜんぶ、あなたが
つくったの?
そうよ。
しょうらいは、
じぶんでお店(みせ)を
ひらきたいんだ。
がんばってね！

First girl: すてき！
これぜんぶ、あなたが
つくったの？
How beautiful!
You made all of these?

Second girl: そうよ。
That's right.

Second girl: しょうらいは、
じぶんでお店をひらきたいんだ。
Someday I want to open my own store.

First girl: がんばってね！
Good luck!

STREET / ROAD

みち、ドウ

ex. 道路* (どうろ) - road; highway
ex. 道辺* (みちべ) - roadside
ex. 柔道* (じゅうどう) - judo

`ヽ` `ヽ` `ソ` `ソ` `ソ` `首` `首`
`首` `首` `首` `道` `道`

ねえ、この**道**
ほんとうに
あっているの?

道はあっている!
はずなんだけど…
なぁ…..

やっぱり、
道にまよったかなぁ…

ぜったい
まよって
いるわよ!

| Girl: ねえ、この道
ほんとうに
あっているの?
Are you sure this
is the right road? | Boy: 道はあっている!
はずなんだけど…
なぁ…
This is the right road!
I think so, anyway... | Boy: やっぱり、
道にまよったかなぁ…
Um, we might be on the
wrong road...

Girl: ぜったいまよって
いるわよ!
We're definitely lost! |

室

ROOM

むろ、シツ

ex. 室内* (しつない) - in the room
ex. 教室 (きょうしつ) - classroom
ex. 室外 (しつがい) - outdoors

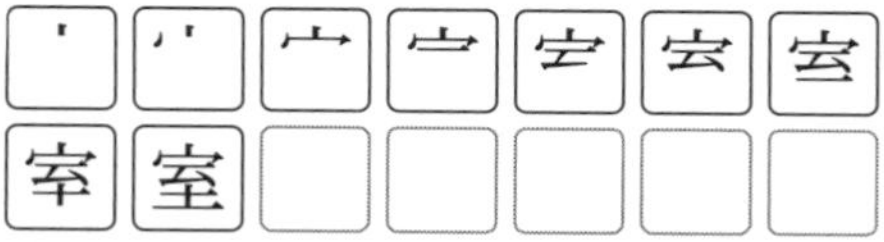

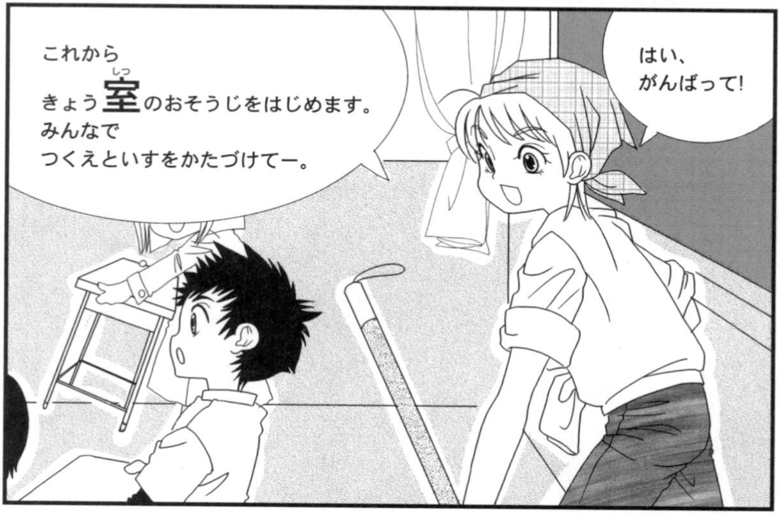
これから
きょう室のおそうじをはじめます。
みんなで
つくえといすをかたづけてー。
はい、
がんばって!

Teacher: これからきょう室のおそうじをはじめます。みんなでつくえといすをかたづけてー。

All right, it's time to clean our classroom.
Everyone move your desks and chairs.

(In Japan, students—not janitors—are responsible for the upkeep of their classrooms. At the end of the schoolday, the children mop the floors and clean the windows. These activities teach the importance of teamwork and help instill school pride.)

はい、がんばって！
That's right, attaboy!

EYE

め、モク

ex. 目ぐすり (めぐすり) - eyedrops
ex. 目途* (めど) - outlook
ex. 科目* (かもく) - school subject

おはよう...

わっ！

どうしたの?!
目のまわりが
すごくはれてるよ。

きのう、すごくなける
えいがをたくさん
みちゃって...

なかないで！
もっと目のまわりが
はれちゃうよ。

Schoolgirl: おはよう...
　　Morning...

Classmate: わっ！
　　どうしたの?！目のまわりが
　　すごくはれてるよ。
　　Whoa! What happened? Your eyes
　　are all puffy.

Schoolgirl: きのう、すごくなける
　　えいがをたくさんみちゃって...
　　I watched a real tear-jerker of a movie
　　yesterday...

Classmate: なかないで！もっと目の
　　まわりがはれちゃうよ。
　　Don't cry now! Your eyes will get worse.

元

ORIGIN

もと、ゲン、ガン

ex. 元祖* (がんそ) - originator; pioneer
ex. 元日 (がんじつ) - New Year's Day
ex. 元気 (げんき) - healthy

一	二	テ	元			

ごちゃ ごちゃ
まぁっ!
こんなに
ちらかして!

元どおりに
かたづけなさい!
きちんとよ?!
わかったなら
へんじをして!
は…はーい。

ごちゃごちゃ
(roughhousing noises)

Mother: まぁっ！
こんなにちらかして！
My goodness! What a mess!

Mother: 元どおりにかたづけなさい！
きちんとよ？！わかったなら
へんじをして！
Put everything back the way it was!
You hear?! Answer me if you understand!

Boys: は…はーい。
Y...Yes.

COMPANY

社

やしろ、シャ

ex. 社長 (しゃちょう) - company president
ex. 社会科* (しゃかいか) - social studies
ex. 社 (やしろ) - Shinto shrine

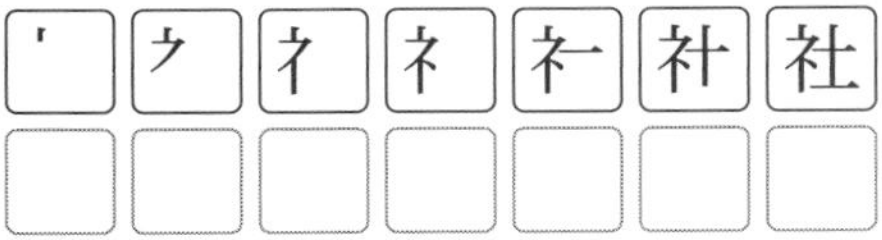

きょうの社(しゃ)かいのじゅぎょうは…
かい社(しゃ)けんがくです!
かい社
!!
社(しゃ)ちょうさんです!
こんにちはー

Teacher: きょうの社かいのじゅぎょうは…
For today's social studies lesson...

Teacher: かい社けんがくです！
...we will visit a company!

Sign: かい社 (Company)

Teacher: 社ちょうさんです！
There's the company president!

Students (in unison): こんにちはー
Hello-ooo!

EVENING

ゆう

ex. 夕方 (ゆうがた) - evening
ex. 夕日 (ゆうひ) - evening (setting) sun
ex. 夕刊* (ゆうかん) - evening newspaper

ノ　ク　夕　□　□　□　□
□　□　□　□　□　□　□

きょうはきれいな
夕ひね。

おかあさん、みて。
かげがこんなにながいよ。

Mother: きょうはきれいな夕ひね。
It sure is a beautiful evening.

Boy: おかあさん、みて。
かげがこんなにながいよ。
Look, mom. Our shadows are really long.

NIGHT

よ、よる、ヤ

ex. 夜空 (よぞら) - night sky
ex. 夜中 (よなか) - midnight
ex. 夜食 (やしょく) - midnight snack

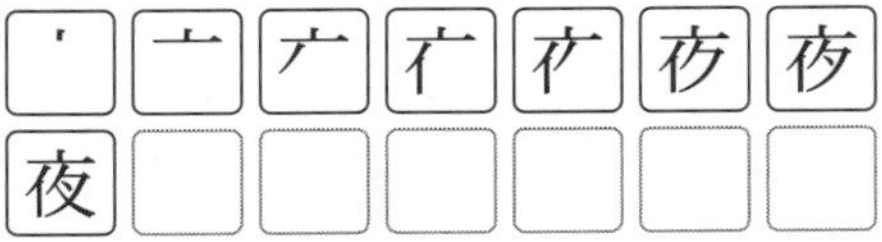

ﾉ　亠　广　疒　夜　夜　夜
夜

なんでオバケって
夜くらいしか
でてこないのかしら...

なんだ、
そんなこと
かんたんだよ！

ひるまでてきても
こわくないもん。
だから
夜なんだよ。

それも
そうね。

Girl: なんでオバケって夜くらいしか
でてこないのかしら...
I wonder why ghosts only come out
at night...

Boy: なんだ、そんなことかんたんだよ！
That's an easy one!

Boy: ひるまでてきてもこわくないもん。
だから夜なんだよ。
They wouldn't be scary when it's
bright out, so they come out at night.

ドキッ (sound of shock)

じー... (sound of staring)

Girl: それもそうね。 That makes sense.

TAKE THE TEST!

The Japanese Language Proficiency Test has been held annually throughout the world since 1984. Administered by the Japanese government and the nonprofit Japan Foundation, the test evaluates and certifies the proficiency of non-native speakers of Japanese. There are four levels to the examination: Level 4 for beginners, Level 3 for intermediate students, Level 2 for those who are functionally literate in Japanese, and Level 1 for experts.

This book features 80 of the kanji students need to know to pass Level 3 of the JLPT. Subsequent volumes in Manga University's *Kanji de Manga* series will help students prepare for the higher levels.

For more information about the Japanese Language Proficiency Test, including examination locations in your country, please visit the Japan Foundation's "JLPT Communications Square" website at http://momo.jpf.go.jp/jlpt/e/about_e.html.

Kanji de Manga

みんさん
しゅくだいの
作ぶんは
かいて
きましたか？
はーい!!!

PRACTICE SECTION

KANJI INDEX

The 80 kanji featured in this volume of *Kanji de Manga* are indexed here based on their *on-yomi* and *kun-yomi* readings. This makes it easy to look up any kanji for which you know a pronunciation but cannot remember how the character is written. Because most kanji have more than one reading, you will find those characters listed multiple times in this index.

あ

あ(う)	会	12
あお	青	13
あお(い)	青	13
あか	赤	14
あか(い)	赤	14
あか(るい)	明	15
あき(らか)	明	15
あき	秋	16
あ(く)	空	55
あ(ける)	空	55
あさ	朝	17
あし	足	18
あに	兄	19
あね	姉	20
あゆ(む)	歩	21
ある(く)	歩	21

い

い(う)	言	22
いえ	家	23
いぬ	犬	24
いもうと	妹	25
いろ	色	26

う

うお	魚	27
うし	牛	28
うた	歌	29
うた(う)	歌	29
うみ	海	30
う(る)	売	31
う(れる)	売	31

お

おお(い)	多	32
おと	音	33
おとうと	弟	34
おな(じ)	同	35
おも(う)	思	36
オン	音	33

か

カ	家	23
カ	歌	29
カ	夏	70
カ	花	74
ガ	画	37
カイ	会	12
カイ	海	30
か(う)	買	38
かえ(す)	帰	39
かえ(る)	帰	39
カク	画	37

ガク	楽	60
かざ	風	40
かぜ	風	40
かた	方	41
かみ	紙	42
から	空	55
かんが(える)	考	43
ガン	元	88

き

キ	帰	39
きっ	切	45
ギュウ	牛	28
ギョ	魚	27
キョウ	兄	19
キョウ	京	44
キョウ	強	66
き(る)	切	45
キン	近	62

く

ク	口	46
ク	工	48
クウ	空	55
くち	口	46
くろ	黒	47
くろ(い)	黒	47

け

ケ	家	23
ゲ	夏	70
ケイ	兄	19
ケイ	京	44
ケン	犬	24
ゲン	言	22
ゲン	元	88

こ

コ	古	80
コウ	考	43
コウ	口	46
コウ	工	48
コウ	広	78
ゴウ	強	66
コク	黒	47
こころ	心	49
こた(え)	答	50
こた(える)	答	50
こと	言	22
ゴン	言	22

さ

サ	茶	64
サ	作	65
サイ	切	45
さかな	魚	27
サク	作	65

し

シ	姉	20
シ	思	36
シ	紙	42
シ	止	68
ジ	字	61
ジ	地	26
シキ	色	86
シツ	室	89
シャ	社	67
シュ	手	16
シュウ	秋	52
シュウ	週	76
シュン	春	
ショウ	少	54

ショウ	正	58
ショク	色	26
し(る)	知	53
シン	心	49

す

すく(ない)	少	54
すこ(し)	少	54

せ

セイ	青	13
セイ	正	58
セキ	赤	14
セツ	切	45

そ

ソウ	走	73
ソウ	早	75
ソク	足	18
そら	空	55

た

タ	多	32
た	田	56
タイ	台	57
ダイ	弟	34
ダイ	台	57
ただ(しい)	正	58
ただ(す)	正	58
た(つ)	立	59
た(てる)	立	59
たの(しい)	楽	60
たの(しむ)	楽	60
たり(る)	足	18
たる	足	18

ち

チ	知	53
チ	地	61
ちか(い)	近	62
ちから	力	63
チャ	茶	64
チュウ	昼	77
チョウ	朝	17
チョウ	鳥	69
チョウ	町	83

つ

つく(る)	作	65
つよ(い)	強	66
つよ(まる)	強	66

て

て	手	67
デ	弟	34
テイ	弟	34
テン	店	84
デン	田	56

と

トウ	答	50
トウ	冬	79
ドウ	同	35
ドウ	道	85
と(まる)	止	68
と(める)	止	68
とり	鳥	69

な

なつ	夏	70

に

ニク	肉	71

ね

ね	音	33